Words of Encouragement

The Sayings of Jesus

Designed by Harold George

First published in Great Britain in 1991
PALM TREE PRESS
Rattlesden, Bury St Edmunds,
Suffolk IP30 0SZ

ISBN 086208 157 2

Contents

Why are you so agitated, and why
are these doubts rising in your
hearts? Yes, it is I indeed. Touch
me and see for yourselves.
Their joy was so great that they
still could not believe it, and
stood there dumbfounded.

Luke 24: 38-41

You ought to be happy because of what you have seen me do, and heard me say. Many prophets and holy people longed to see what you have seen, and hear what you have heard, but could not.

Matthew 13: 16, 17

One day, some people challenged
Jesus, "Why is it that John's
disciples and the disciples of the
Pharisees fast, but your disciples
do not?"
Jesus replied, "Do friends of the
bridegroom refuse to eat at the
wedding feast? Why should they be
sad as long as he is still with
them? The time will come when the
bridegroom will be taken away from
them, and then, on that day, they
will fast."

Mark 2: 18-21

At the moment you grieve, but your grief will be turned to joy. A woman in childbirth suffers, because her time has come; but when she has given birth she forgets the suffering in her joy that a child has been born into the world.

So it is with you: you are sad now, but I shall see you again, and your hearts will be full of joy, and that joy no one shall take from you.

John 16: 21, 22

When you fast, don't do it publicly,
as the hypocrites do: they pull long
faces, and try to look miserable, so
people will feel sorry for them.
When you fast, try to appear happy
and contented so that no one will
suspect you are fasting—only your
Father in heaven will know.

Matthew 6: 16

As Jesus was speaking, a woman in
the crowd called out,
"Happy is the mother who gave you
birth and nursed you."
Jesus replied,
"Happy rather are those who hear
the word of God and obey it."

Luke 11: 28

Don't be afraid of those who can kill only your body—but can't touch your soul.

Matthew 10: 28

Well done, good and faithful servant; you have shown you can be faithful in small things, I will trust you in greater; come and join in your master's happiness.

Matthew 25: 21 and 23

There will be more rejoicing in heaven over one sinner who repents than over ninety-nine who have not strayed and do not need to repent.

Luke 15: 7

I have told you everything I have received from my Father so that you may have the full measure of my joy within you.

John 17: 13

Do you think the work of harvesting
will not begin until the summer ends
four months from now?
Look around you! Vast fields of
human souls are ripening all around
us, and are ready now for reaping.
The reapers will be paid good wages
and will be gathering eternal souls
into the granaries of heaven. What
joys await the sower and the reaper,
both together!

John 4: 35, 36

Happy are those who have not
seen me and yet believe.

John 20: 29

Live within my love. When you obey
me you are living in my love, just as
I obey my Father and live in his love.
I have told you this so that you will
be filled with joy. Yes, your cup of
joy will overflow!

John 15: 9-11

Be at peace with one another
Mark 9:50

I give you a new commandment:
love one another.
Just as I have loved you,
you also must love one another.
By this love you have for one
another, everyone will know
that you are my disciples.

John 13:34

Greater love has no man than
this, that a man lay down
his life for his friends.

John 15:13

Peace be with you.

John 20:19

Peace I leave with you; my
peace I give you. I do not give
to you as the world gives.
Do not let your hearts be
troubled, and do not be afraid.

John 14: 27, 28

For God so loved the world that
he gave his only Son, that
whoever believes in him shall not
perish but have eternal life.

John 3:16

The man who loves his life will
lose it, while the man who hates
his life in this world will keep
it for eternal life.

John 12:25

You have heard it said, "You shall love your neighbour and hate your enemy." But I say to you, love your enemies and pray for those who persecute you, so that you may be sons of your Father who is in heaven.

Matthew 5: 43, 44

Blessed are the peacemakers,
for they shall be called
sons of God.

Matthew 5:9

Do you truly love me?

John 21:15

You shall love the Lord your God
with all your heart,
and with all your soul,
and with all your mind.
This is the great and first
commandment.
And the second is like it:
you shall love your neighbour
as yourself.
On these two commandments
depend all the law and the prophets.

Matthew 22: 37-40

I have told you all this
so that you may find peace in me.
In the world you will have
trouble but be brave:
I have conquered the world.

John 16:33

As the Father has loved me,
so I have loved you.
Remain in my love.
If you keep my commandments
you will remain in my love,
just as I have kept my Father's
commandments and remain in his love.
I have told you this
so that my own joy may be in you
and your joy be complete.

John 15: 9-11

If you love only those who love
you, what good is that? Even
scoundrels do that much!
If you are friendly only to
your friends, how are you
different from anyone else?
Even the heathens do that!
But you are to be perfect,
even as your Father in heaven
is perfect.

Matthew 5: 46-48

Whoever accepts my commandments
and obeys them is the one who loves me;
My father will love whoever loves me;
I too will love him and reveal myself
to him.

John 14:21

A man who was covered with leprosy came along to Jesus, and fell on his face to the ground and begged Jesus, "Lord, if you are willing, you can make me clean." Jesus reached out his hand and touched the man. "Of course I will," he said, "be healed." And immediately the leprosy left him.

Luke 5: 12, 13

Some men brought to Jesus a paralytic, lying on a mat. When Jesus saw their faith, he said to the paralytic, "Take heart, son; your sins are forgiven." At this, some of the teachers of the Law

mumbled to themselves, "This man is blaspheming!" Knowing their thoughts, Jesus said, "Why do you entertain such evil thoughts in your hearts? Which is easier: to say 'Your sins are forgiven' or to say 'Get up and walk'? But so that you may know that the Son of Man has authority on earth to forgive sins —" then he said to the paralytic, "—Get up, take up your mat and go home." And the man got up and went home.

When the crowd saw this, they were filled with awe: and they praised God, who had given such authority to men.

Matthew 9: 2-7

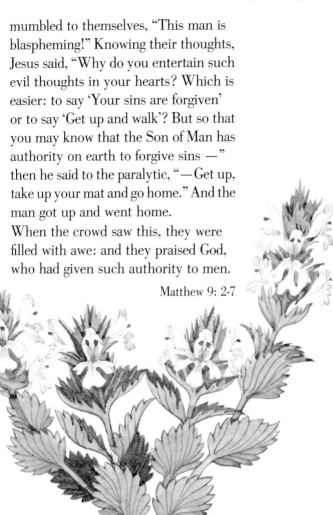

One sabbath day when Jesus was teaching in the synagogue, there was a woman who for eighteen years had been possessed by a spirit that left her handicapped; she was bent double and quite unable to stand upright. When Jesus saw her, he called over and said, "Woman, you are healed of your sickness" and he laid his hands on her. At once she straightened up, and she glorified God. And all the people were overjoyed at all the wonders Jesus worked.

Luke 13: 10-13

Jesus reached Lazarus' tomb: it was a
cave with a stone to close the opening.
Jesus said, "Take the stone away."
Then he prayed, "Father, I thank you
for hearing my prayer. I know indeed
that you always hear me, but I speak
for the sake of all those who stand
around me, so that they may believe it
was you who sent me."
When he said this, he cried out in a
loud voice, "Lazarus, here! Come out!"
The dead man came out.

John 11: 38, 39, 41-44

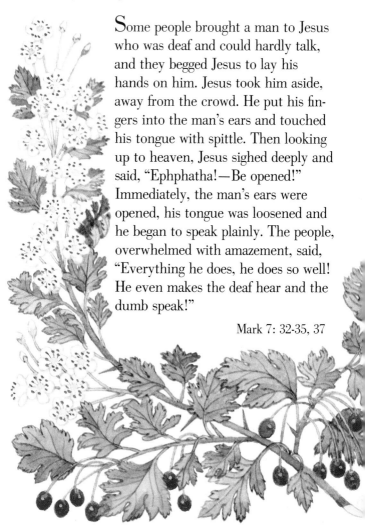

Some people brought a man to Jesus who was deaf and could hardly talk, and they begged Jesus to lay his hands on him. Jesus took him aside, away from the crowd. He put his fingers into the man's ears and touched his tongue with spittle. Then looking up to heaven, Jesus sighed deeply and said, "Ephphatha!—Be opened!" Immediately, the man's ears were opened, his tongue was loosened and he began to speak plainly. The people, overwhelmed with amazement, said, "Everything he does, he does so well! He even makes the deaf hear and the dumb speak!"

Mark 7: 32-35, 37

Jesus said to the man lying beside
the Sheep Pool, who had been ill for
thirty-eight years, "Do you want to
be well again," Then he said, "Get up,
pick up your sleeping-mat and walk."
The man was cured at once, and he
picked up his mat and walked away.
Afterwards, Jesus told him, "Now
that you are well again, be sure not
to sin any more, or something worse
may happen to you."

John 5: 5, 8, 9, 14

Your faith has made you well; go in
peace and be healed.

Mark 5: 34

Jairus, the leader of the synagogue, came and fell down before Jesus, pleading with him to heal his little daughter. "She's at the point of death!" he said in desperation, "Please come and lay your hands on her and make her live." While Jesus was on his way to Jairus' house, news came that the little girl had died. Jesus said to Jairus, "Don't be afraid. Just trust me."

Jesus went into Jairus' house and spoke to the people there:

"Why all this weeping and commotion? The child isn't dead — only asleep!"

Taking her by the hand, he said to her,
"Get up, little girl!" And she jumped
up and walked around!

Mark 5: 22 ff

A woman who had been sick for twelve
years with internal bleeding came up
behind Jesus and touched the fringe
of his cloak, for she thought, "If I
only touch him, I will be healed."
Jesus turned around and spoke to her.
"Daughter," he said, "all is well!
Your faith has healed you." And the
woman was well from that moment.

Matthew 9: 20-22

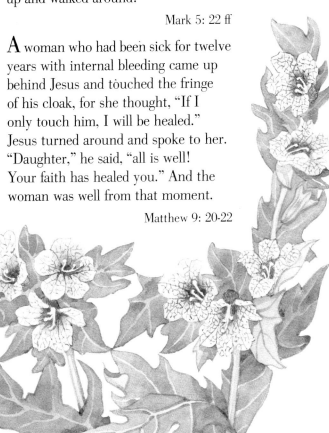

Two blind men followed along behind
Jesus, shouting, "O Son of King David,
have mercy on us!" Jesus asked them,
"Do you believe I can make you see?"
"Yes, Lord, we do."
Then he touched their eyes and said,
"Because of your faith it will happen."
And suddenly they could see!

Matthew 9: 27-29

I have come into the world to give sight
to those who are spiritually blind and
to show those who think they see that
they are blind.

John 9: 39

Heal the sick, and tell them
"The kingdom of God is near you."

Luke 10: 9

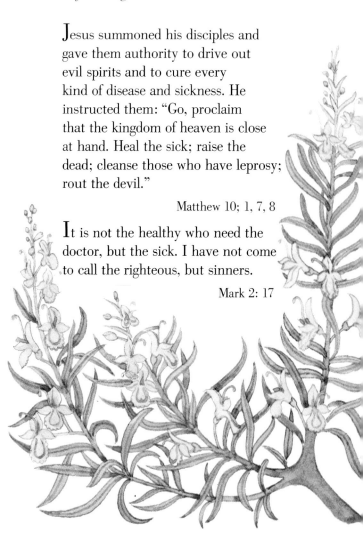

Jesus summoned his disciples and gave them authority to drive out evil spirits and to cure every kind of disease and sickness. He instructed them: "Go, proclaim that the kingdom of heaven is close at hand. Heal the sick; raise the dead; cleanse those who have leprosy; rout the devil."

Matthew 10; 1, 7, 8

It is not the healthy who need the doctor, but the sick. I have not come to call the righteous, but sinners.

Mark 2: 17

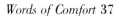

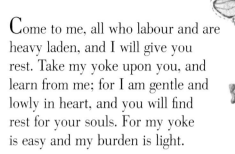

Come to me, all who labour and are heavy laden, and I will give you rest. Take my yoke upon you, and learn from me; for I am gentle and lowly in heart, and you will find rest for your souls. For my yoke is easy and my burden is light.

Matthew 11:28-30

If the Son makes you free, you will be free indeed.

John 8:36

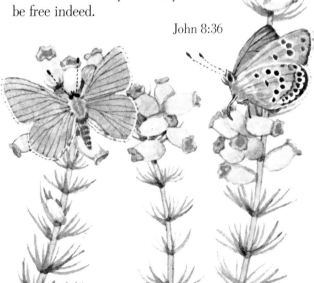

Ask, and it will be given you;
seek and you will find; knock
and it will be opened to you.
For everyone who asks receives,
and he who seeks finds, and to
him who knocks it will be opened.

Luke 11:9-10

If anyone thirst, let him come
to me and drink.

John 7:37

Do not be worried and upset.
Believe in God, and believe also
in me. There are many rooms in
my Father's house, and I am going
to prepare a place for you. I
would not tell you this if it
were not so. And after I go and
prepare a place for you, I will
come back and take you to myself,
so that you will be where I am.
You know the way that leads to
the place where I am going.

John 14:1-4

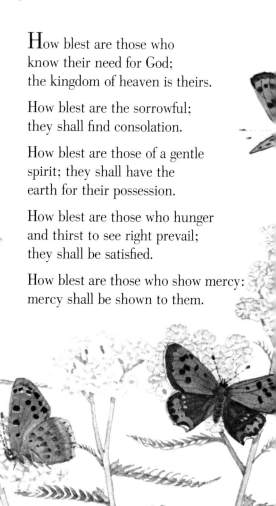

How blest are those who
know their need for God;
the kingdom of heaven is theirs.

How blest are the sorrowful;
they shall find consolation.

How blest are those of a gentle
spirit; they shall have the
earth for their possession.

How blest are those who hunger
and thirst to see right prevail;
they shall be satisfied.

How blest are those who show mercy:
mercy shall be shown to them.

How blest are those whose hearts
are pure; they shall see God.

How blest are the peacemakers;
God shall call them his sons.

How blest are those who have suffered
persecution for the cause of right;
the kingdom of heaven is theirs.

How blest are you when you suffer
insults and persecution and every
kind of calumny for my sake. Accept
it with goodness and exultation, for
you have a rich reward in heaven.

Matthew 5:3-12

For only a penny you can buy two sparrows, yet not one sparrow falls to the ground without your Father's consent. As for you, even the hairs of your head have all been counted. So do not be afraid; you are worth more than hundreds of sparrows.

Matthew 10:29-31

Your faith has saved you.

Mark 10:52

If the world hates you, remember that it hated me before you. If you belonged to the world, the world would love you as its own; but because you do not belong to the world, because my choice withdrew you from the world, therefore the world hates you.

John 15:18, 19

Today you will be with me in paradise.

Luke 23:43

You are sad now, but I will see you again, and your hearts will be full of joy, a joy that no one can take from you.

John 16:22

Take heart; it is I, have no fear.

Matthew 14:27

I am the good shepherd; I know
my own and my own know me, as
the Father knows me and I know
the Father; and I lay down my
life for the sheep.

John 10:14, 15

Do not be afraid.

Matthew 28:10

I did not come to invite virtuous people, but sinners.

Matthew 9:13

I am the bread of life; he who comes to me will never be hungry, and he who believes in me will never be thirsty. And I will raise him up at the last day.

John 6:35, 40

Know that I am with you always:
yes, even to the end of time.

Matthew 28:20